A Saffron Robe

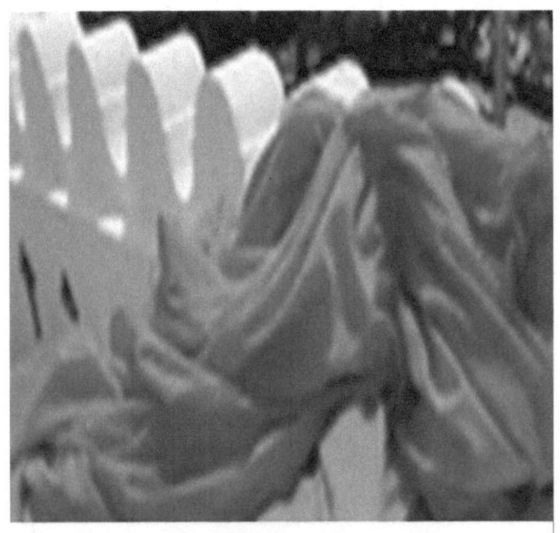

A Saffron Robe

A Chapbook of Poetry

Philippe R Hebert

Philippe R Hebert

AF583182

Copyright© 2024 Philippe R Hebert

ISBN: 978-93-6354-668-4

First Edition: 2024

Rs. 200/-

Cyberwit.net

HIG 45 Kaushambi Kunj, Kalindipuram

Allahabad - 211011 (U.P.) India

http://www.cyberwit.net

E-mail: info@cyberwit.net

No part of this book may be reproduced or transmitted in any form or by any means, electronic, mechanical, photocopying, or otherwise, without the express written consent of Philippe R Hebert.

Printed at Repro.

Bio

Philippe R Hebert is an 81 year old poet, writer, and story teller.

- Book of Vietnam War poems "Elephant Ears and Bamboo Shoots" published by Human Error Publishing
- Poetry Book "A Begging Bowl" published by Human Error Publishing
- Poetry Chapbook "A Saffron Robe" with Cyberwit Publishing
- "A Shoji Screen" published with Cyberwit Publishing
- "A Marshy Pond" published with Cyberwit Publishing
- Published in "Bards Poetry Review 2024"
- Pushcart nominee
- Exit 13 Issue, #29 publish "Tejas"
- Canyon Voices "The Heron" & "The Night Comes Quickly"
- Vietnam War Poetry December 2022 4 poems, April 2024 2 poems
- Spill Words Press January 2023, May 2023, August 2023, May 2024
- Published in The Stillwater Review 2023
- Arts By The People December 2023
- Anthologies "The More I Forget" 2022, & "Nature Knows the Way" 2023
- Poetry Nation "Peace & Serenity" & "Retrospectively"
- Published in Transfusion Blood Services Journal December 2010
- Published Handbook for Savings in Freight & Logistics

- Working on a book for children titled “Fritz, My Bestest Friend”
- Over 60 Manufacturing Publications in Modern Material Handling and T&D
- A Case Study at Lehigh University
- Active member of Newton NJ Writers Roundtable
- Active member of Poetry At The Barn
- Active member of Newton NJ Library writers and Poets

Table of Contents

A Saffron Robe

It's almost a daily occurrence
to see monks with shaved heads,
a begging bowl,
and a saffron robe.

The saffron robe signifies a
renunciation of all earthly things,
selfless karma, penance, piousness and the
shaved head connotes a desire for peace.

Since the saffron robe has no pockets a
begging bowl serves two purposes, it
collects the coins from daily begging and
to hold the days rice for meals.

So the saffron robe signifies a renunciation
of material things a dedication to selflessness
and humility while in pursuit of peace
and atonement while on earth.

White Cranes

Two white cranes stand motionless
against the background of darkening woods
hunting food
as if posing for a shoji screen.

The image, stark in the twilight
and reflected on the water's edge.
The sky is tinted shades of yellow and gray
as if forecasting happiness and good fortune.

A thirsty doe leads the small herd
slowly and cautiously approaching
the need for water and the lush grasses
overcomes their inherent fear.

The Night Comes Quickly

The night comes quickly
and then the sounds
seem to be amplified.
Sitting on the patio
alone with my thoughts.

I cant help but wonder
what did I accomplish?
have I achieved anything?
did I make a difference today?
Is the world a better place?

Reading sometimes breeds inspiration
so jotting down words which are
conscripted for future use
images appear and some vaporize
while others remain.

Paint those images with words,
splash them on the page
return later to refine them
but for now it's enough
to capture them as if they might float away.

But for now
the night gobbles up the inspiration
leaving no telltale sign
that anything occurred
just a blank page.

Some day

Sitting on the patio of my old adobe house
in a pueblo high atop a mountain.
morning has yet to shed its light.

It's cool and a bit foggy,
a mountain cat calls and a dog barks
almost as if answering.
Steaming rich black coffee in hand
ready to meet the new day.

What will be encountered?
What shall we do?

Just put off everything for now
and light the first
cigar of the day.
See the blue gray cloud of smoke
and smell the pungent sweet aroma.

Now just lean back and
enjoy the coffee and cigar
life will take care of itself for now.

The leaving of the cities
and simply being "in the moment"
is harder than you think.
But then again it's wonderful to simply
exist in this heaven I've created.

I can think and write later today…
perhaps in the cantina
or under the old tree in the plaza.
But no rush… it will be
there tomorrow too.

So many words float about
some landing on a page.
Maybe it will be this blue smudge
that nobody will read.
But that’s ok maybe – someday.

Life In Two Parts

In the town center
a small nook
holds a coffee shop
selling home made tarts

If you're early enough
you can get one
with the pitch black brew
banana, blackberry, or raspberry

Sit and enjoy
life's being lived
at almost a slow motion pace
slow but constant get things done

Women with infants
men with horse or donkey
hawking flowers, sugar cane, bananas
arthritic hands and stooped backs

Some look 60 but are 30
some are 30 and look 60
"I counted my years and found that I have less time to live
from here on than I have lived up to now" someone said.

If life is in two parts
the first we've lived
then the second part with realization
we don't have much left

These thoughts only happen
when we're older and sit in silence
contemplating life
or the sins of our past

A Handful of Minutes

There is just a handful of minutes
left in this lifetime
so we sit and think
as the predawn passes
a slight light emerges

Frogs crooks, crickets chirp
and the loons call sadly.
The smell of honeysuckle is strong
and we think of a reoccurring question…
what have we accomplished?

And what do we aspire to?
It's too late in life
to begin a Magnus Opus (as G. Lighcap says)
but then again, lifelong projects
begin with the first step.

Some poetry has been written,
we are not an artists, so
what is left for us
but to write again?

We come from tragic stock
The Acadians cast off
into the Atlantic
families are separated. (the story of Evangeline)

Some fortunate landed
in Newfoundland, Quebec,
then others in Louisiana.
Our heritage was from Quebec.

An ancestor
Philippe Rene Hébert
was the first to settle
in Quebec.

Old Fool Move Along

Some days are better than others
aches and pains but
nothing to complain about
beyond the autumn of our lives.

Without a backward glance
at our age
sad and joyous memories
floods the mind

It's simple to wallow
in misery and sadness
force ourselves
to rise above the muck and mire

Easy to dwell on short comings
that life dealt out
the unrequited love but
we do reap what's been sown

Recall the rice farmers
and the sugar cane harvester
are our lives much worse
then why so piteous
poor fool
pick yourself up and move along!

Don’t listen
family, friends, doctors
tell you
don’t drink, eat wisely, and exercise

You know how you feel
you know what's good and bad
smoking is not good
so you gave it up

Scotch lets you relax
allows for random thinking
there's no DT's
just a mellow peace

With inhibitions removed
free thought comes alive
you remember when
and can even see the future

Don't pity yourself
so went your parents and grandparents
everyone goes down that path
why shouldn't you...you're not so special
so pick yourself up
and get along old fool.

Old Man

Today I was lamenting my age and limited capabilities
and in passing through downtown near the circle
I saw an old man wearing a coat and hat
Bent over double and shuffling without a soul to help.

How dare we lament and seek sympathy
whilst we can at least stagger but upright.
My mind wanders and imagines his life past and present
where did he come from and where might he be going?

Surely his past must have been monotonous and difficult
bent under a burden of packages or bricks on his back.
The black Irish cabby hat speaks of blue collar
the thin leather coat says no, I was an accountant.

Walking up Main street in the downtown
says he lives nearby, probably a one bedroom
apartment without A/C over a Law firm
probably feeds himself Chinese from down the street.

Rent at $800 a month and utilities at $175
Two meals a day and a bottle of wine.
Now exhaust his total retirement income
and Social Security of $1400 per month.

It's no wonder that he's bent over double
and shuffles. There is no future
only today and yesterday's.
And we lament our state in life.
For shame. For shame.

We have the mindset that
foreigners like the French and British
retirees are suffering and scraping to get by.

Well I'm here to tell you that they
enjoy a better life style that our retirees.

The pensions of French and British retirees
are adjusted much more frequently than our retirees.
So the image of the French Legionaries
is a very real depiction of the elder in the USA.

Just the cost of medicines and food
consume most of their income
leaving little for rent.

And now, post pandemic, the food costs
have sky rocketed along with transportation costs.
And yet the elderly have not received
an income adjustment.

So don't pity
the poor French legionaries
Think instead of the American elder
that buys Alpo because its cheaper
than beef or pork for a dinner.

So again, for shame, that an American
senior citizen has to struggle
to pay rent or buy food after working life long.
After all, we are still one of the riches country in the
world.

And we lament our state in life.

Kyoto in April

The Sakura blooms are at their peak
bright pinks and white connote purity
cover the trees as if a blanket
enjoy the sight because in 10 days they'll be gone.

Reach out and caress the blossoms
how delicate and smooth
each petal is states "Live in the Present"
small clusters of individual beauty.

And at night
if you listen closely
you can hear each blossom
shout out their very presence

Blossoms exist in the 10 days of festival of Sakura.
But the tastes of Sakura exist all year long
Tempura, Yakitori, Teriyaki
With mounds of sticky rice

The smells of Sakura are of Spring itself
Everything is clear, clean, new
Subtle cherry blooms fragrance
Barely there almost indistinguishable, delightful.

Asian Eyes

Eyes that challenge
and dare you to come forward
Eyes that drill into your mind and soul
Eyes that read your very thoughts

Eyes that invite you, if you dare
and boldly state I'm as hot as molten lava.
You could get burnt
or immersed in a molten tryst

Asian eyes that are guarded
and demure while saying so much.
A sudden flash at what's perceived
to be less than completely honest

So then, Asian eyes like ebony
what's to be your next move?
Eyes that can shield intent
while soliciting your intent.

Eyes that beg for love
but are guarded against potential hurt.
Eyes that challenge
yet dare you to come forward.

Neng So Dear

Exotic Asia
Where East meets West
Captured mind and heart
So sophisticated and older

Music of Piaf & Newley
Mendez & Aznavour
<u>Getz</u>, Gilberto

Nights alone
Then nights sitting
In a graveyard or on a dock
Virginia Beach watching
Phosphorus from the sea waves

I touched your hair
But wanted more
Scared to lose a friend
To gain a lover

Eating rice and chorizo
Drinking wine
And smoking Salem's
Pack after pack

Playing those tunes
Over and over
Talking in sexual innuendoes
With feelings laid bare.

The hormones of a 20 year old
Matching and exceeding
A woman of 25 or so
But who's counting now?

But back then
It was scandalous
Remembering
Makes me blush.

The short pitch black hair
Cinnamon color of your skin
Eyes darker than your hair
Eyes that see into and sear my soul

So intense you inhibit me
left to doubt
Can I, should I
You are so worldly
And I'm a child.
You have such a presence
Even 10 years after
Wife by my side
I take and light 2 Salem's at once
And no one even flinches

I become yours again
For that time together
I am helpless
Student or slave
Good bye.

Hibiscus

A tropical beauty
swaying in the sun
an invitation

Dahlias

Where dahlias grow
There was a bridge and
a lonely heart sat

White Cranes

Like a shoji screen
two white cranes stand motionless
fishing for minnows

El Condor

El condor passa
oh how majestic in flight
carrion eater

You are

Scent of jasmine
you are whispers of my heart
and shouts in my brain

Writing

Pouring forth my heart
and emptying of my soul
how freeing it is

Bird of Paradise

Aptly named
only one look
the distinct design and color
says loud and clear
you are not of this earth

An ethereal beauty
orange, yellow, blue, or purple
a symbol of beauty and grace
or perhaps freedom
but doesn't survive shade

Hibiscus

Another tropical beauty
with a myriad of colors
scarlet, yellow, pink, violet
basking in the sun

The summer breeze
causes the hibiscus to sway
against dark green of leaves
like an invitation of sorts

Imaginings

My mind's abuzz
as I surround myself
with imaginings
of flowers and shrubs

I envision myself
sitting among clumps of bamboo
the wind stops
everything is quite

The sun warms
everything it touches
even the smooth dark rocks
seem to respond to the warmth

The Cohasset Mansion

The good doctor
bargained the purchase
of a Cohasset Massachusetts mansion
with the aid of
the Bishop of Boston in 1952.

On 130 acres of remote
wooded property
a sanatorium for alcoholics
and high profile addicts.

Photos show the mansion house
caretakers cottage, stables,
paddocks, pool hall,
and swimming pool.

The doctors and his family
resided in the all 3 floors of the west wing
replete with onyx fireplaces, mahogany furniture,
leaded stained-glass windows

The balance encompassed 13 bedrooms,
dining hall, recreation hall, kitchen and
a great room.

The medical staff resided in the
mansions center and
was staffed by
two male nurses and one female nurse,

A hunchback assistant named Johnny
accompanied
the good doctor everywhere
and even ate meals with the family.

The good doctor
ran and administered the sanatorium.
he was the doctor
and sometimes the patient.

A Safe Place

Sitting in an Old Town canoe
In the early morning
Waters lapping the canoe's green sides
Paddle across the gunnels
Waiting for peace and
The first rays of sunshine
Lakeside are pines and spruces
A woodpecker doing his job
A doe and her fawn
Approach the lakes edge
For a drink
I retrieve the thermos for coffee
No human sounds
Except the one's I make
Silence
To mend my soul

Acadia

There's a bend
in the shallow river
water rushes by
the granite boulders

Granite boulders everywhere
so still, so silent
amidst the water
only the sound of the wind

In the spring
so green and lush
the wind is mild
water still cold from melting snow

In the autumn
leaves so vibrant, its blinding
the smell of fall can't be forgotten
leaves rushing and cracking

When you're old
you're young again
run as before
but in your mind.

Summers in Acadia

Memories of youth
camping on the beach
under a parachute tent
a case of Narraganset
a bottle of Vat 69
Buffy Saint Marie
with Canadian girls by our sides
We did not know, what we did not know.

At summers end
fire flies and honeysuckle
semi dark by 9pm
reading and sharing Frank Yerby
touchy feely evenings at 15.
Exploring while listening
to Doo Wop on the crystal radio.

Tolling of Bells

There is nothing these days
as dramatic as the tolling of bells
to draw attention to death
of ones friends

It seems as if death
sneaks in and passes by
without a whisper

Months pass by before we become
aware of someone's death.
How sad that events such as this
go unnoticed almost as if
they are of no consequence.

Relocate me to a casita
with my dog.
Rice and beans with a side of tortillas
and a block of queso auhmado cheese
I can survive and perhaps even thrive.

Beat The Drum

I beat the drum
in memory of him.
I raise the flag
applaud and
sing his praises.

I remember
and respect
his achievements
I appreciate
heap accolades,
quote and
lead his
posse.
I maintain
that well loved
warm glow for him.
I follow
proudly.

And wonder
who will
raise the flag and
beat the drum
for me?
Who will beat the drum for me? (el pendejo
desconocido*)

*el pendejo desconocido = unknown son of a bitch

Yesterday's Flowers

My mind and memories
are fading like last week's flowers
Who is that?
And how did that saying go?

Like Bill Joel's *"when I wore
a younger man's clothes"*
and why is there so much
wisdom in country music?

There is no safe harbor
from age and the ultimately
grim reaper…grim reaper

My dearest, where have you gone?

Across the kitchen table
from my wife of 55 years
I see the feisty young beauty
with raven black hair and eyes
The smooth cinnamon skin
that turned my eyes and never sought another.

But the image
changes to an older woman
with grey hair and sad eyes
the skin on her neck is now
turkeyed
The cinnamon color
has greyed as well.

She stutters and searches
for words that she spoke for decades
Words so simple but
they elude her now.

Those eyes that were once alive
are now clouded
and stare off to who know where.

I'm losing my love
one piece at a time.
I morn for her
and cry for myself.

It's not fair that that light
should dim in her
and leave me

Who knows where her mind travels to
And I should be with her
as its always been.

But truth be told
I don’t know if I’m sad and lonely
because she’s going off alone
or if because I’m left here alone.

A Thousand Mile Stare

You glide from one world to another
at times there's a notable stumble,
your eyes will cloud over
you might slur your words.

You stop in mid-sentence
searching for the simplest of words
or you begin speaking
mid thought as if I had been in your mind

The most painful
is your mumbled thoughts
while leveling a questioning look
as if to say what's the matter with you?

Then again the helplessness I feel
looking at your trembling hands
while evoking that thousand yard stare
not only battled scared soldiers have that look.

Your disposition has changed
previously alert and ready to stand your ground
now aggressive and with defiance
malice in your eyes and tone

Where have you been
that so dramatically changed you
what happened to the friendly open person
Where did you lose her during your wanderings
Where Did You Lose Her

Willow in the Wind

As the light fades
from her eyes
And the cinnamon color of her skin
turns yellow
I think back over the years
and wonder what became of the time.
The volatility has slowly vaporized.
It seems like only yesterday
that we were young
It seems like yesterday
that we existed
only for each other.

Her eyes held only love and admiration
mine held only devotion and adoration for
the young brown girl I held.
She was so petite and delicate
that it seemed a squeeze
would break her
But 54 years have passed
and I love her all the more.
So tiny, petite, and delicate
but she wont break
she will bend like the
willow in the wind.

How can I go on
without my lover,
my partner,
my best friend?
Time has lead us
to this fork
she'll tread one path
and I will live alone on another.

We will talk as before
but only in my mind.
Go softly my willow in the wind
And I'll stay here alone.

www.ingramcontent.com/pod-product-compliance
Lightning Source LLC
LaVergne TN
LVHW091242150826
845673LV00003B/1251

* 9 7 8 9 3 6 3 5 4 6 6 8 4 *